A Note to Parents

Dorling Kindersley Readers is a compelling program for beginning readers, designed in conjunction with leading literacy experts, including Dr. Linda Gambrell, Director of the School of Education at Clemson University. Dr. Gambrell has served on the Board of Directors of the International Reading Association and as President of the National Reading Conference.

Beautiful illustrations and superb full-color photographs combine with engaging, easy-to-read stories to offer a fresh approach to each subject in the series. Each *Dorling Kindersley Reader* is guaranteed to capture a child's interest while developing his or her reading skills, general knowledge, and love of reading.

The four levels of *Dorling Kindersley Readers* are aimed at different reading abilities, enabling you to choose the books that are exactly right for your child:

Level 1 – Beginning to read
Level 2 – Beginning to read alone
Level 3 – Reading alone
Level 4 – Proficient readers

The "normal" age at which a child begins to read can be anywhere from three to eight years old, so these levels are only a general guideline.

No matter which level you select, you can be sure that you are helping your child learn to read, then read to learn!

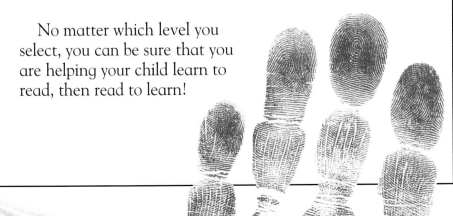

Dorling **DK** Kindersley

LONDON, NEW YORK, SYDNEY, DELHI, PARIS,
MUNICH, and JOHANNESBURG

Edited and Designed by
Nimbusbooks

Series Editor Deborah Lock
Senior Art Editor Clare Shedden
US Editor Regina Kahney
Production Shivani Pandey
Picture Researchers Brenda Clynch,
Andrea Sadler
Illustrator Peter Dennis
Jacket Designer Sophia Tampakopoulos
Indexer Lynn Bresler

Reading Consultant
Linda Gambrell, Ph.D.

First American Edition, 2001
00 01 02 03 04 05 10 9 8 7 6 5 4 3 2 1
Published in the United States by DK Publishing, Inc.
95 Madison Avenue, New York, New York 10016

Color reproduction by Colourscan, Singapore
Printed and bound in China by L Rex Printing Co., Ltd.

The publisher thanks the following for their kind permission
to reproduce their photographs:
c=center; t=top; b=bottom; l=left; r=right

Agence France Presse: 47br; **Brown Brothers:** 4bl, 19tr; **Corbis:** 16, 24tl,
36tl; Bettmann 20-21, 23; Duomo 21cr; Minnesota Historical Society 12b;
Roger Ressmeyer 25; Michael S. Yamashita 13tr; **Mary Evans Picture
Library:** 10; **Hulton Getty:** 13br; **The Granger Collection, New York:** 15br;
Ronald Grant Archive: 15tr.; **The Guardian, Prince Edward Island:** 41tr,
41br, 47bl; **H Keith Melton Collection:** 12tl.; **Image Bank:** Archive Photos
20cl; J. Carmichael 34tl; **Metropolitan Police Museum:** 38bl; **Metropolitan
Police Service:** 9br, 39tr; **Richard Neave:** 30tl, 30cl; **Frank Nowikowski:**
permission of Juan Vucetich Police Museum, La Plata, Argentina 7tr, 9tr,
11tr; **Stephen O'Brien:** 46tl; **New York City Police Museum:** 19br; **Science
Photo Library:** 2, 29b; Simon Fraser 46bl; David Parker 44; Alfred Pasieka
45; Harvey Pincis 37; Dr. Jurgen Scriba 42, 43tr; **Frank Spooner Pictures:** G.
Bassignac/Gamma 35; **Telegraph Colour Library:** Robert Clare 4tl, 49;
Topham Picturepoint: 11br, 18, 31tr; **Western Mail and Echo Ltd, Cardiff:**
26, 28, 33; **Dr. Brian Widdop of the Medical Toxicology Unit Laboratory:**
36cl; **Jerry Young:** 31bl, 32tl, 32bl, 32br.

Jacket: **Assistant Divisional Officer Derek Thorpe and the
Fire Investigation Unit at Acton Fire Station:** front br;
Gettyone.Stone: Kevin Irby front cover background;
Peter Dazeley front cover bl.; Leland Bobbe back cover tl.

see our complete
catalog at
www.dk.com

Contents

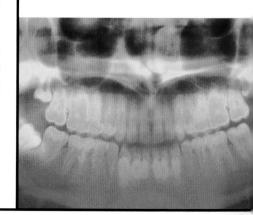

DORLING KINDERSLEY *READERS*

PROFICIENT **4** READERS

CRIME BUSTERS

Written by Andrew Donkin

A Dorling Kindersley Book

A murderer in Argentina was the first killer to be caught by fingerprints. See page 6.

Read how a bank robber was trapped by a helpful spirit from beyond the grave! See page 12.

Learn how one of America's most infamous gangsters was finally sent to jail. See page 18.

Crime meets science

Everybody loves a good murder mystery. But to police detectives, solving crimes is a way of life.

Whenever a crime is committed, detectives visit the scene and search for clues that may bring the criminal to justice. All the clues, or evidence, are analyzed in a laboratory.

Today, police scientists can tell some amazing things from the tiniest clues – even the fictional detective Sherlock Holmes may not have noticed them!

This book features six true stories about crime busting and how vital evidence revealed "who dunit" to the detectives on each case. ❖

Watch as the identity of a mysterious human skull is revealed. See page 26.

Discover how a man's pet cat sent him to prison for life. See page 40.

Read how police scientists can find vital clues in a victim's body to solve a crime. See page 34.

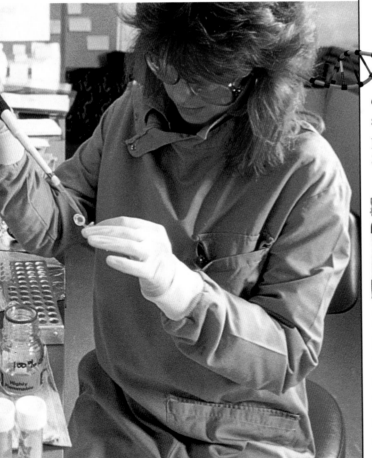

Necochea
Necochea was a typical, quiet Argentinian village. People relied on farming for their income.

The mark of a killer

When Police Inspector Eduardo Alvarez walked into the small South American village, he felt everyone watching him very closely.

It was 1892 and the inspector had been sent to Necochea (NEE-oh-KOE-chee-uh), Argentina, from the nearby city of Buenos Aires.

A terrible double murder had been committed. The local police had been unable to solve the crime, so they had asked for help from the city's police force. Inspector Alvarez was chosen to investigate the case.

"The two bodies were found in the hut of a woman named Francesca Rojas," the local policeman told Alvarez.

"Do you have any suspects?" Alvarez asked.

"The woman claims that her boyfriend, a farmer named Velasquez, is the murderer," explained the local policeman. "We have questioned him for days, but he insists that he is innocent. We have no eyewitnesses and no other evidence against him. Can you help us, Inspector?"

"I hope so," replied Alvarez. "First, I need to examine the hut."

Police Inspector Alvarez
Eduardo Alvarez was dedicated to his work. He followed new developments in crime detection very closely.

Police expertise
In Argentina, during the 1800s, rural police often sought the help of city police to solve complicated crimes.

One room
In rural Argentinian villages, in the past and today, whole families often live in just one room. Sometimes they have curtains dividing the room for privacy.

The local policeman led Alvarez through the stifling afternoon heat toward a small, creaky wooden shack at the end of the town. "This is the hut where the crime took place. Everything has been left just as it was," said the policeman.

Inspector Alvarez stepped into the gloom inside and slowly looked around the entire shack from floor to ceiling. At the back, he saw the bloodstains from the murders.

As he turned around to leave the hut, Alvarez's eyes were drawn to a red mark on the door. He looked closer. The mark was a bloody fingerprint.

In the late 1800s, fingerprints were not used to solve crimes – few people even knew about them. But Alvarez had been reading about fingerprints in the work of Argentinian police expert Juan Vucetich. He realized that this could be his best chance to catch the murderer.

But there was no way to lift the fingerprint from the door. How could he get it back to police headquarters? After a lot of thought Alvarez found a way.

Juan Vucetich
Vucetich was head of the Statistical Bureau of Police in Buenos Aires. He was trying to develop a system that used fingerprints to catch criminals.

Finding prints
Today, experts dust surfaces with a fine powder to find fingerprints left by the oils on people's fingers.

Unique prints
Everyone's fingerprints are unique – nobody else will have a fingerprint exactly the same as yours.

When Velasquez, the chief suspect, was brought into Alvarez's room at police headquarters, he was surprised to find a wooden door leaning against the wall. Alvarez had borrowed a saw and cut the entire door from its hinges!

Alvarez coated the man's fingertips in red ink. He then pressed each fingertip on to a piece of paper. The red prints on the paper showed the shapes made by the ridges and furrows on Velasquez's fingertips. Alvarez studied the results under a magnifying glass.

Four types
Fingerprints are divided into four types – arch, loop, whorl, and composite. Composite have features of two or more types.

"None of them match," announced Alvarez. "Release him and bring in Francesca Rojas, the owner of the hut."

Arch

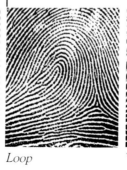
Loop

Whorl

Composite

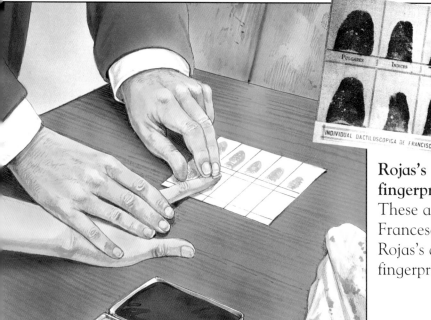

Francesca Rojas watched Alvarez put red ink on her fingertips and examine the prints closely, all the time wondering what the policeman was up to.

Alvarez saw immediately that the woman's left thumb print was a perfect match with the one on the door! Rojas was so surprised and scared that she immediately confessed to the terrible crimes.

Quick-witted Inspector Alvarez became the first detective to use fingerprints to solve a murder. ❖

On file
Police departments worldwide keep fingerprint records. When they find a print at a crime scene, they compare it with the prints in their records.

Trademark
It was the eye in the middle of Pinkerton's trademark that gave him and his men the name "Private Eye." The nickname was soon used for all private investigators.

The helpful ghost

Allan Pinkerton's reputation stretched across America. It was a reputation for solving crimes.

Pinkerton had set up the world's first private detective agency in 1850, and he had been on the trail of criminals ever since.

Now, he had been called to a small town in California to catch a bank robber.

Inside a typical late 19th-century bank

The bank in the town had been held up and the bank teller had been killed during the raid.

The thief – now a murderer as well – had made a clean getaway with $130,000. This would be worth over five million dollars today!

The local sheriff was unable to solve the crime, so he called in Pinkerton to help him. Although there were no witnesses to the robbery or murder, Pinkerton soon became suspicious of a man named Alexander P. Drysdale.

When questioned, Drysdale proclaimed his innocence strongly. But he had been seen lurking around the bank just before the raid.

Despite his suspicions, Pinkerton could do nothing without any firm evidence. For a while the case went nowhere – until he got some help from beyond the grave!

Modern security
Banks in the mid 1800s had vaults to store money, but the vaults did not have the high-tech computer-coded locks and reinforced doors that are used in today's banks.

Bounty hunters
Criminals were often caught by bounty hunters in return for money. One dollar in 1850 was equivalent to about 40 dollars today.

Surveillance
Today's private investigators have a lot of equipment to help them, including long-lens cameras and cassette recorders. Pinkerton's men had to rely on their wits and early cameras.

Pinkerton had sent for three assistants to help him. When they arrived, the local townsfolk were amazed by the appearance of one of the detectives, a young man named Green.

"He's the spitting image of the dead bank teller!" exclaimed one of the shopkeepers.

This gave the quick-thinking Pinkerton a brilliant idea. Pinkerton instructed one of his assistants to ask their suspect, Drysdale, to take a walk with him. Just before sunset, the two men strolled out to Rocky Creek – a place the locals said was haunted.

As the two men walked along, a dreadful moaning sound seemed to be coming from ahead of them. Suddenly, a dark figure stumbled out of the twilight. It was Green, made up to look like the ghost of the murdered bank teller!

Drysdale let out a scream of terror and ran straight for home! Pinkerton's suspicions seemed to be correct. But this was not enough. He knew that Drysdale needed to confess to the robbery and to killing the bank teller.

Pinkerton had an idea to make him do just that.

Police line-up
Police use line-ups to identify suspects. They find people who look like the suspect and then ask the witnesses to pick out the suspect from the group.

Infamous bank robbers Bonnie and Clyde became famous in 1930s America for robbing many banks and killing 32 people in two years.

Civil war
During the Civil War (1861–1863), Pinkerton was head of the Union's Secret Service. He used his detective skills to act as a spy and to get information from the Confederates.

President Lincoln
Pinkerton helped to save the life of President Abraham Lincoln during a plot to assassinate him in 1861.

For the next three nights, Pinkerton had his "ghost" make a terrifying midnight appearance at Drysdale's home. Pinkerton and his assistants would sneak into the back garden. Exactly at the stroke of midnight, the "spook" would appear from behind the bushes and then stumble around the garden letting out a horrible wailing sound.

Each night, Pinkerton saw Drysdale watching in terror from an upstairs window.

Soon Drysdale began to have terrible nightmares and was hardly able to sleep, even in the daytime! After four days of ghostly hauntings, Pinkerton decided that his suspect was ready for the final part of his master plan.

Pinkerton arrested Drysdale and insisted on taking the terrified man back to the bank – the scene of the robbery and murder.

When Drysdale entered the building, Green jumped out at him, still disguised as the ghost. Drysdale fainted to the floor. When he came around, he couldn't wait to confess his crimes – robbery and murder – in the desperate hope that the fiendish ghost would leave him alone.

Thanks to a very helpful "ghost," Pinkerton had found his man. ❖

Badge of office
Pinkerton's men carried a badge of office to prove they were private detectives.

Eliot Ness
Born in 1902, Eliot Ness became well known during the 1920s for leading a team that fought to break up the trade in illegal liquor.

The Untouchables

One day in September 1929, Special Agent Eliot Ness was called into the office of Chicago's district attorney. The 26-year-old detective had a growing reputation among his fellow officers as a hard-working cop with a cool head. He was going to need it, because Ness was about to be given the most dangerous assignment of his life.

"We want you to take down Al Capone," said the district attorney. "The government wants you to cripple his operation." Ness let the news sink in for a few seconds and then swallowed hard. This would be a tough and risky job.

Al "Scarface" Capone was Chicago's Public Enemy Number One – he was their gangland Mafia boss. The ruthless gangster inspired fear in the general public, rival gangs, and the city's police force.

Capone's two main weapons were bribes and bullets. Cops who would not take his money and do what he ordered might find themselves caught in a hail of gunfire instead.

Ness had been serving as a special agent in the Prohibition Bureau of the Department of Justice for a while, but this would be an entirely different assignment. Ness would be singling out Capone.

Al Capone
Capone was born in New York in 1899. During a fight, he received a razor slash across his face, which earned him the nickname "Scarface."

Violin cases were used to hide guns.

Paul Robsky
Robsky was a telephone tapper – he listened in on Capone's conversations.

Joe Leeson
Leeson was able to trail a suspect without being spotted.

Lyle Chapman
Chapman was a genius at solving puzzles and problems.

Capone feared no one. Once he even sent 20 men with machine guns to raid a police station!

The sharp-suited gangster always traveled around the city in his own special car. It weighed over seven tons because of the armor-plated frame and bullet-proof windows.

On February 14, 1929, Capone had arranged the shooting of seven members of a rival gang. This is now known as the St. Valentine's Day Massacre.

Eliot Ness agreed to take on Capone. He chose his squad of officers carefully, picking only those he felt he could trust not to take Capone's bribes. When they were offered money, they had to be "untouchable." The name stuck.

Ness chose Lyle Chapman, Mike Chapman, Barney Cloonan, Mike King, Joe Leeson, and Paul Robsky. Each of Ness's six Untouchables was chosen for his specialist skills. Together they were unbeatable.

Mike Chapman
Mike Chapman was strong and fit. He used to play professional football.

Barney Cloonan
Cloonan was a very strong Irishman who towered over and frightened gangsters.

Mike King
King had an amazing memory. He was called the "Memory Man."

Capone made a lot of his profits brewing illegal (bootleg) liquor in secret distilleries. Ness found that by the time his men sledghammered their way into each distillery, the criminals had escaped. Ness solved this problem by smashing into the dens using a 10-ton truck with a huge steel snowplow on the front. Now he could simply smash his way into the middle of the gangsters' headquarters using his new "gang-buster!"

In their first year, the Untouchables raided and closed down over 25 illegal distilleries, together worth over one million dollars to Capone.

Capone tried to bribe Eliot Ness, just as he had tried with many other detectives. He offered Ness $2,000 per week to stop the raids. Ness refused Capone's offer.

Volstead Act
This act was introduced in 1919. It made the sale of liquor illegal. This period became known as Prohibition.

Making liquor
During Prohibition, gangs made and sold liquor secretly. The picture below shows federal agents pouring away illegal wine they had found.

Soup kitchen
When Capone decided he needed some good publicity, he set up a soup kitchen. He gave free soup to 5,000 poor and unemployed people daily.

When the raids continued, Capone got serious. He hired a hit man to "rub out" Ness and get rid of him once and for all!

When Ness heard about Capone's plan, he made sure that he carried a photograph of the hit man with him everywhere he went, so he could spot him in a crowd. Ness did finally spot him, and, after a car chase through the streets of Chicago, the would-be assassin was thrown in jail.

Ness also survived other attempts on his life by Capone's agents. They took a shot at him during a drive-by shooting, wired a bomb to his car, and even tried to run him over!

Undeterred, the Untouchables continued their raids, knocking out more and more of Capone's illegal distilleries. Capone's wealth and lavish lifestyle were under threat.

Soon Al Capone – one-time king of Chicago – was in trouble. While Ness had been striking at Capone's gangster empire, tax officials, led by Frank J. Wilson, had been busy investigating Capone's secret financial affairs. On October 17, 1931, the gangster was finally found guilty of tax evasion and sent to prison for 11 years. On his release, Capone was a broken man. ❖

Alcatraz
Capone served four years in this notorious prison. The prison is on an island in the San Francisco Bay.

Frank J. Wilson
Wilson found three black books showing Capone's profits from his gambling rackets. This was enough evidence to prove Capone had been evading his taxes.

Little Miss Nobody

When two builders arrived for work one morning in 1989, they had no idea that they were about to unearth a murder mystery that was over a decade old.

The men had been hired to carry out some improvements in the garden of 29, Fitzhamon Embankment in Cardiff, Wales. Their first job was to dig a drainage ditch across the garden. After about an hour, one of the men dug into a roll of thick carpet buried deep under the earth.

They agreed to dig out the whole thing. The men quickly dug around the carpet, trying to ignore the horrible smell of decay.

When they unrolled the carpet, the two men had a terrible shock. Hidden in the middle of the roll was a complete human skeleton! The flesh had long since decayed. The rotting remains of the victim's clothes hung in tatters on the yellowing bones.

State of decay
Generally, a body that is left exposed to air will decay eight times more quickly than a body buried in earth. The fatter a person is, the faster the body will decay!

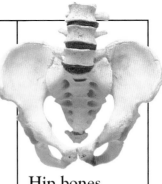

The police were at the crime scene very quickly. A hidden body meant only one thing – that a crime had been committed. They immediately began a murder investigation.

But the detectives had a difficult task on their hands. There was no identification on the body. Carefully, they pieced together the few clues they had, starting with the most obvious. Men and women have different-shaped skulls and hip bones. This skeleton was a woman. Her teeth were examined and they showed she was under 20 years old.

Hip bones
It is possible to tell the sex of a skeleton by studying the hip bones. Men's hips, like those above, are narrower and deeper than women's.

Telltale teeth
The biting surface of teeth wear away with age. Young teeth have a bumpy surface.

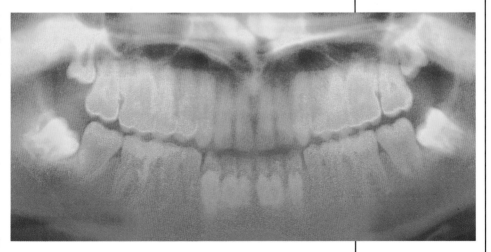

Richard Neave
Neave is a medical illustrator working at Manchester University, England.

King Midas
Neave recreated the face of King Midas from the king's 2,700-year-old skull. Legend has it that anything Midas touched turned to gold.

Now they knew they had found the body of a young woman, but this didn't help them much. Hundreds of people had lived at 29, Fitzhamon Embankment over the years. Had she been a tenant, a visitor, or had her murderer lived in the house?

The police turned to Richard Neave for help. They asked Neave to take the skull and recreate the dead woman's face!

Richard Neave, one of Britain's most talented medical illustrators, had become well known for rebuilding the faces of skulls to show what the person would have looked like when he or she was alive.

He was used to doing this with famous figures from history like King Midas, but not with murder victims.

Neave started by making a perfect plaster cast of the skull. Next, he inserted two plastic eyes into the eye sockets.

Using a small drill, Neave made holes at special places on the skull. He inserted small sticks into each hole and pushed them in to a depth that showed the thickness of muscle tissue at that point on the skull.

Mikhail Gerasimov (above left) Gerasimov was a Russian scientist who explored the methods of facial reconstruction in the 1920s. His work has included recreating some of the faces of the earliest humans.

Materials Neave casts the skulls in a material called alginate, which is made from seaweed.

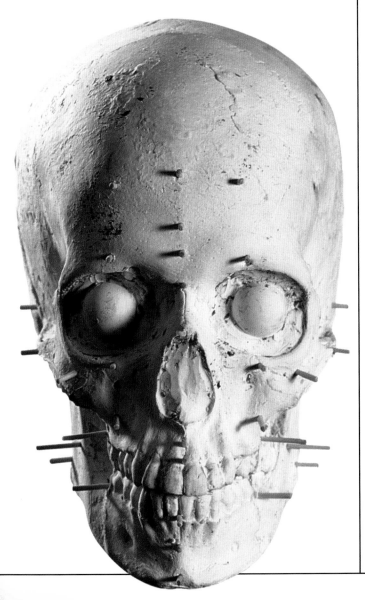

31

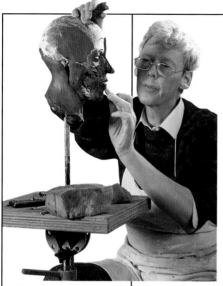

Now Neave was ready for the hardest part.

With great care, he began to build up the face with thick brown clay, using his expert knowledge to recreate the face from the skull.

Recreating muscle
Neave adds all the facial muscles to the face in clay before he creates the skin texture on top.

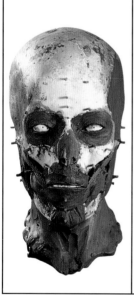

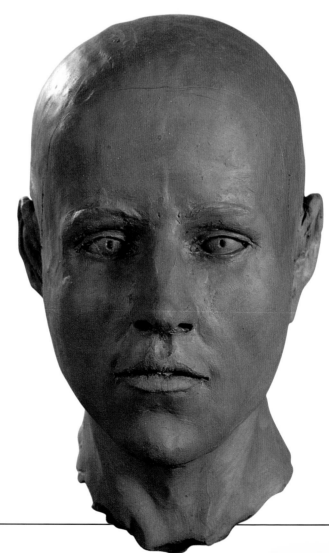

The nose was always a particularly difficult part, and Neave took his best guess at its probable shape. When the shape of the face was finished, Neave smoothed clay into the texture of a young woman's skin. Finally, he guessed at a hair style for the murder victim.

Karen Price
Karen was a 15-year-old school girl. She had run away from a children's home. It was Karen's social worker who recognized the head.

Detectives gave pictures of the lifelike head to national newspapers and television channels, appealing to the public for help in identifying the young woman. Within two days, a lady telephoned to say that she recognized the face as being Karen Price. It was the breakthrough the police needed.

The investigation ended with two men going to prison for Karen's murder – all thanks to Neave's work turning an unknown skull back into a recognizable human face. ❖

Karen's killers
In February 1991, Alan Charlton and Idris Ali were found guilty of Karen's murder and sent to prison.

Isolated places
Murder victims are sometimes dumped in the woods in the hope the bodies will not be found easily or quickly.

The telltale taco

Late one night in 1992, three police cars stood parked by the roadside with their blue emergency lights shining into the darkness.

A passing motorist had reported seeing a body lying by the side of the quiet back road outside the California town of Oceanside.

The police had moved in to investigate and now they had a murder case on their hands.

Before the body was even touched, scene-of-crime officers (SOCOs) carefully examined the entire area. They took photographs of the victim and where she had been found before they moved her body.

While they worked, other uniformed officers searched the surrounding area looking for the murder weapon. They taped off the area to ensure vital evidence was not trampled, contaminated, or destroyed.

After asking around, the police still had no witnesses, no motive, and no idea where to start looking for the killer. With no clues to go on, the investigation was nearly over before it had begun. The detectives were hoping the autopsy report might give them a lead.

SOCOs
The crime scene is usually examined by specially trained experts called scene-of-crime officers, who spend hours carefully hunting for clues with special equipment.

Protective clothing
SOCOs wear protective hats, gloves, suits, and shoes to ensure they do not contaminate evidence.

Mortuary
Before an autopsy, dead bodies are kept in drawers in a cool room called a mortuary. An autopsy is an examination to find out how a person died.

Stomach fluids
The stomach contains a substance that dissolves food. The less dissolved the food, the shorter the time it has been in the stomach.

The next day, the medical examiner – a special doctor – began the autopsy, dictating her findings into a tape recorder as she worked. "The cause of death was a blow to the head," said the doctor.

Next, she examined the contents of the victim's stomach, a routine part of every autopsy. This is done to find out if the victim has been poisoned. But in this case, the check revealed something else.

"Stomach contents show that the victim's last meal was a Mexican taco," noted the doctor, "and I'd say it had been eaten less than one hour before her death."

The doctor's report gave the detectives a place to start their investigation. Had someone seen the victim buying or eating her last meal?

Medical examiner analyzing food from the victim's stomach to help estimate the time of death.

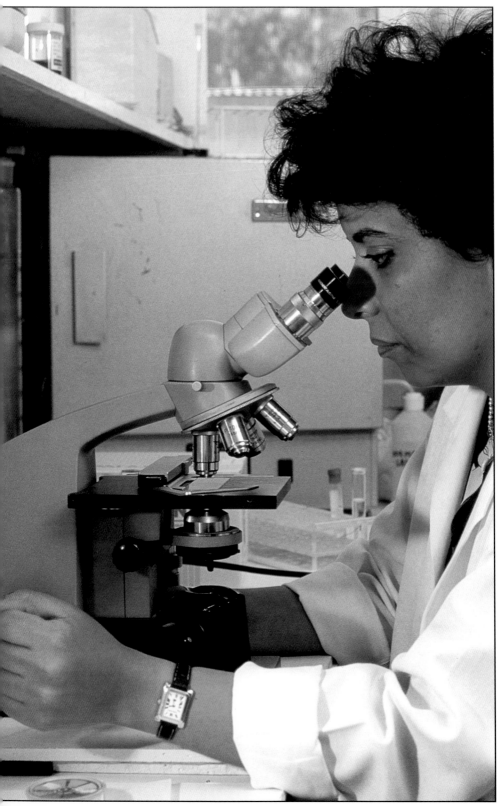

Recognizing faces
The police keep photographs of criminals in mugshot books. People can look through these books to see if they recognize anyone in them.

The detectives began to visit taco restaurants that were less than one hour's drive from where the victim had been found.

At each restaurant, they showed an artist's impression of the woman to waitresses and other staff. After only four restaurants, they got the break they needed. A waitress recognized the picture.

First book
This is the first mugshot book, created by Frenchman Alphonse Bertillon at the end of the 19th century.

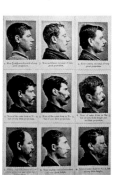

38

"Yeah sure, I remember her," said the waitress. "She bought some tacos here, then she went over to the bar across the street." The detectives wasted no time in questioning the bar's staff.

"Yeah, she was in here the day before yesterday. Just after lunchtime. Saw her leave with one of our regulars," explained the bartender. "She in trouble?"

The bartender knew the name of the man who had left with the murder victim. The detectives went straight to his home, where they found him watching television. When the detectives searched the man's car, they discovered the victim's handbag in the trunk. Realizing he was trapped, the man quickly confessed to murder.

The killer had been caught by his victim's last lunch! ❖

Impressions
It is very difficult to create an accurate likeness of someone. Likenesses made from identikits and artist's impressions are used to give an impression only. They are shown to the public in the hope someone will recognize the person.

Identikit
An identikit picture is made from strips showing eyes, noses, jawlines, mouths, ears, and hairlines.

Cat detective

Shirley Duguay had been missing for seven months before her body was finally found. On May 6, 1995, two hikers were out walking in thick woodland on Prince Edward Island, Canada, when they suddenly stumbled on a shallow grave.

Realizing what they had discovered, the hikers rushed to telephone the police.

Local police had feared the worst since Shirley disappeared from the small town. Just four days after she vanished, her car had been found abandoned in woods only eight miles from her home. The car had bloodstains on the seats.

Now that Shirley's body had been found, the police scientists were able to confirm that the blood in the car belonged to her.

The police were determined to catch her killer – and they strongly suspected that they already knew who it was. Detectives were almost certain that Shirley's boyfriend, Douglas Beamish, was responsible. Beamish had a history of bad behavior and had threatened Shirley in the past. But Beamish denied having anything to do with the murder. Could the police prove otherwise?

Securing the scene
A crime scene is roped off with tape, so people do not enter the area. If it is outside, a tent is erected to protect the area from the weather.

Shirley Duguay
When she died, Duguay was 32 years old. She had three children and had lived with Beamish for nine years.

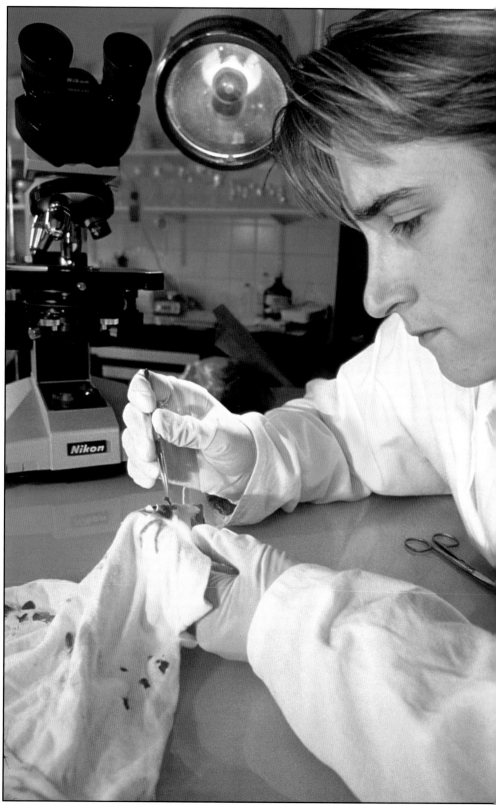

Police had found a man's brown leather jacket also stained with the victim's blood in the car. They believed it belonged to Douglas Beamish, but couldn't prove it.

Now that the case was reopened, they sent the jacket back to their police lab for more tests.

"The blood definitely belongs to the victim, Shirley Duguay," the scientists reported. "The only other thing we found were some long, white cat hairs." At first, the news seemed disappointing, and the detective in charge sat frustrated, flicking through the case notes. Then he remembered something.

"Hey," he called to his colleagues. "When I questioned Beamish, there was a big white cat at his home. I think it was called Snowball, a real friendly tom cat."

Was this the lead they needed?

A scientist analyzing bloodstains on a shirt.

Hair analysis
A person has the same DNA in all his body tissues. So it is possible to tell if strands of hair and spots of blood belong to the same person.

Blood analysis
Scientists can analyze blood and tell if two samples are from the same person, even when the samples are found years apart.

Alec Jeffreys
In 1984, English scientist Professor Alec Jeffreys discovered that every person has a different and unique DNA fingerprint.

Unique strand
By breaking down the components of living tissue, scientists can reveal a strand of DNA unique to that person or animal.

Model of DNA strand (right)

Human hair can be matched to people by a technique known as DNA fingerprinting. Could the same be done for cat fur?

Professor Alec Jeffreys discovered DNA fingerprinting in 1984. Everybody in the world has a different DNA fingerprint – no two people's are the same. DNA is contained in a person's blood, skin, saliva, sweat, and hair. DNA is a more accurate way of identifying criminals than fingerprints.

The detectives used the internet to find an expert on animal DNA. They soon came across scientist Stephen O'Brien, an expert on cat DNA working in Maryland. They contacted him and explained their problem. "I don't think animal DNA has been used in a law court before," said O'Brien, "but we can try."

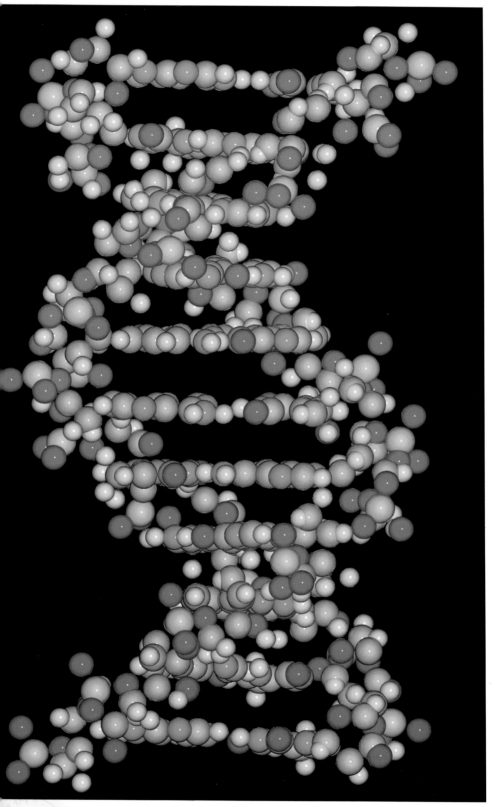

Stephen O'Brien
O'Brien is chief of the Cancer Research Laboratory in Frederick, Maryland. He has worked on many criminal investigations since this case.

DNA bands
The sequence of sections of DNA looks a bit like a computer barcode.

"The first thing I need you to send me," O'Brien explained to the detectives, "is a blood sample from Snowball the cat, and some of the white cat hairs that were found on the jacket."

Detectives rushed both samples to O'Brien's lab so he could start his tests. O'Brien extracted a sample of DNA from the blood sample and the pieces of hair, and then created a DNA fingerprint for both samples. One week later, the detectives had a telephone call from O'Brien.

"It took a lot of work," said the happy scientist, "but we did it. We created DNA profiles for the blood sample and for the hairs – and they're a perfect match!"

The police had proved that the bloodstained jacket had come into contact with Snowball the cat. This evidence pointed the finger of guilt firmly at Douglas Beamish.

Stephen O'Brien was called as an expert witness at Beamish's trial and the killer was sentenced to life in prison – the first criminal ever caught by a cat. ❖

Innocent?
Even after he was found guilty, Beamish still insisted he was innocent. He was sentenced to life imprisonment with no chance of parole.

Animal help
The police often rely on dogs to help them solve crimes. Sniffer dogs are trained to follow a scent. They sniff out criminals and evidence, such as narcotics.

Glossary

Assassination
The killing of a well-known person for political reasons.

Autopsy
The examination of a corpse, or dead body, by a specially trained police doctor to try and discover the exact cause of death.

Black market
The illegal trading of scarce or banned goods. During Prohibition in 1920s America, there was a huge black market for liquor because it was against the law to make, buy, or sell it.

Bootleg
Something that is being sold or traded illegally.

Bounty hunter
Somebody who catches a criminal for a reward.

Bribe
A reward for doing something dishonest or illegal.

Criminal investigation
The examination of events surrounding a crime or criminal activity.

Detective
A plainclothes police officer employed to investigate criminal activities.

Distillery
A place where liquor is made.

District attorney
A lawyer who acts as attorney for the people or government within a specific area or district.

Eyewitness
A person who can describe an event because he or she has seen it happen.

Federal agent
A special kind of detective who works for the U.S. government and can investigate crimes in any part of the country.

Gangster
A member of a close group of criminals who are armed and dangerous. Some gangs belong to a larger organization. For example, the Mafia is made up of several gangs.

Hit man
A person who is asked and paid to kill someone.

Mafia
A large organization of criminals who control their illegal activities and businesses by threats and violence.

Narcotics
Drugs, usually addictive, that cause sleepiness.

Parole
The early release of a prisoner from jail for good behavior.

Prohibition
The period between 1920s and 1930s in America when the sale of liquor was illegal.

Scene-of-crime officer
A specially trained officer who works for the police to collect evidence at a crime scene.

Surveillance
The act of following a person or watching a building to gather information.

Telephone tapping
Using specialist equipment to record telephone conversations.

Witness
Somebody who is called to give evidence in a law court.